Spelling
Workbook

Part 1

My name is Monster.
I can see two more things
beginning with m .
What are they?

mouse

motorbike

What is your name?

My name is _____ .

1

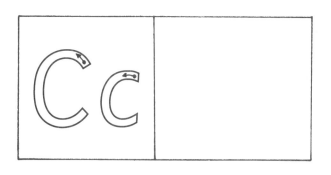

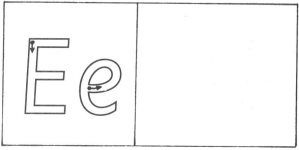

Draw a picture for each letter.

Join the **c** things to the **c** ball.

Join the **e** things to the **e** ball.

Label and colour the **c** prizes blue.

Label and colour the **e** prizes yellow.

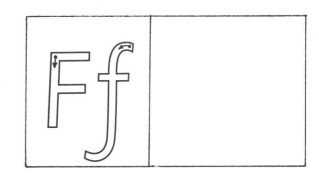

Draw a picture for each letter.

Dd   Ii

Draw a picture for each letter.

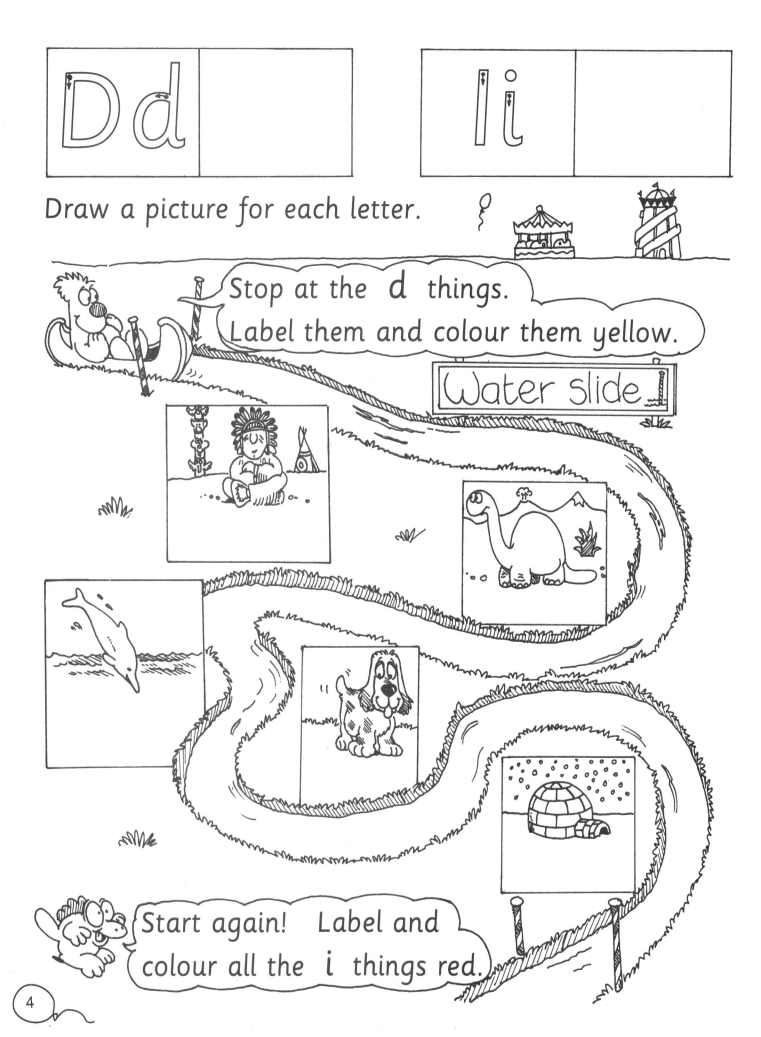

Stop at the **d** things.
Label them and colour them yellow.

Water slide

Start again!   Label and colour all the **i** things red.

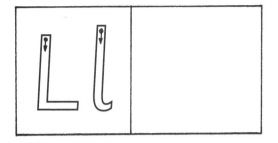

Draw a picture for each letter.

Colour the l animals blue.
Label them.

Colour the m animals red.
Label them.

5

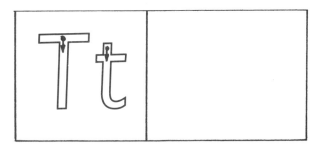

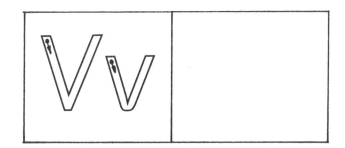

Draw a picture for each letter.

Pick a straw

Label the t things and colour them green.

Label the v things and colour them red.

6

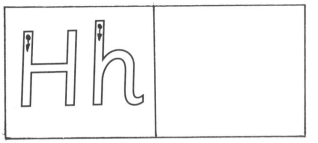
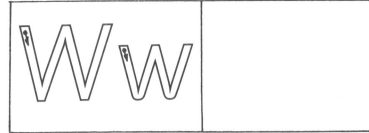

Draw a picture for each letter.

Join the **h** magnet with the **h** things. Label them.

Join the **w** magnet with the **w** things. Label them.

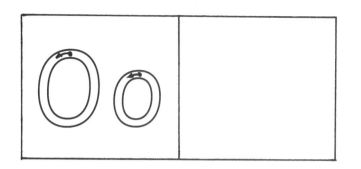
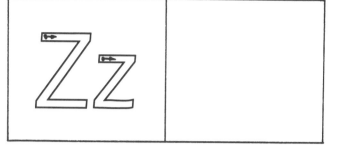

Draw a picture for each letter.

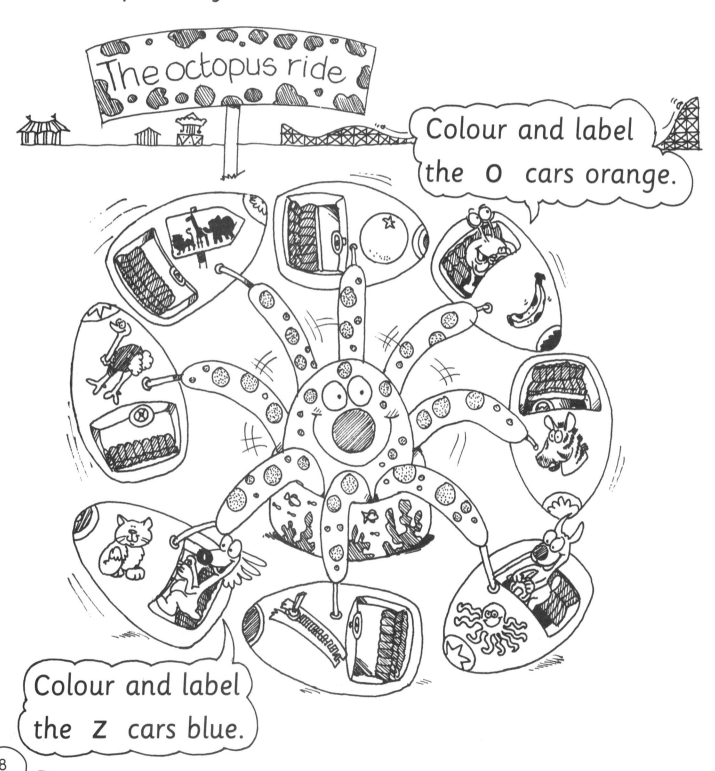

8

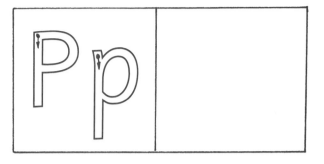

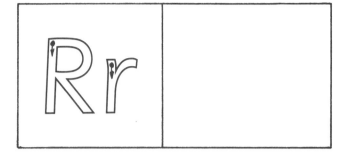

Draw a picture for each letter.

Colour and label the p pennies pink.
Colour and label the r pennies red.

Roll the pennies

Draw and label two more p and r pennies here.

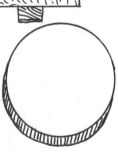

9

Draw a picture for each letter.

Label the **a** balloons and colour them orange.

Label the **g** balloons and colour them green.

Buy a balloon

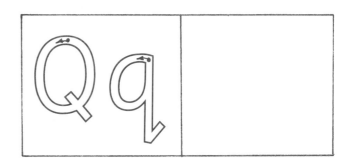

Draw a picture for each letter.

Look at the queue!
Colour the n T-shirts red.
Colour the qu T-shirts blue.

Write qu on my T-shirt.

Write n on my T-shirt.

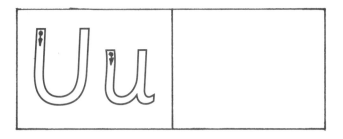
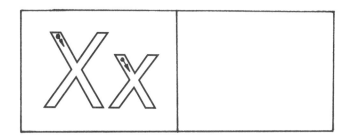

Draw a picture for each letter.

Treasure trail

Join the u words to the umbrella.
Join the x words to the fox.

u

x

up

fox

box

under

six

umbrella

Write some u and some x words
in the treasure chests.

Draw a picture for each letter.

On the lake

Label and colour the **k** yachts blue.

Label and colour the **y** yachts yellow.

13

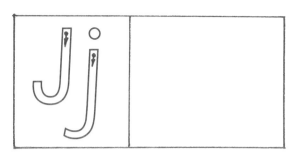 

Draw a picture for each letter.

On Target

Label and colour the **j** pictures.

Label and colour the **s** pictures.

Draw and label another **j** picture
and another **s** picture.

abcdefghijklmnopqrstuvwxyz

Write the letters of the alphabet on the skittles.

Skittles

Colour the skittles that spell your name.

The Juggler

but

cut

nut

fix

six

mix

bat

hut

Colour the ut skittles blue.
Colour the ix skittles red.

Write one of my words under each picture.

16

I have broken my skittles.
Help me fix them.

Make the word	Write the word

 b ut

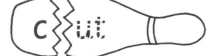 c ut

 h ut

 n ut

 m ix

 s ix

 f ix

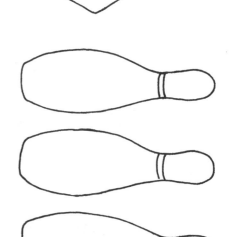

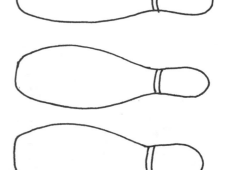

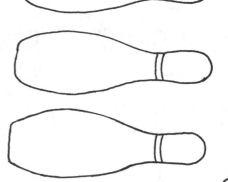

Cover

Darts

Join the darts to match the pictures.
Write the words in the spaces.

sun

hop

top

bun

mop

run

Make a word		Write the word
	op	
	op	
	op	
	un	
	un	
	un	

Cover

Use some **un** and **op** words to finish this sentence.

It is good _____ to _____

and _____ .

19

The Coconut Shy

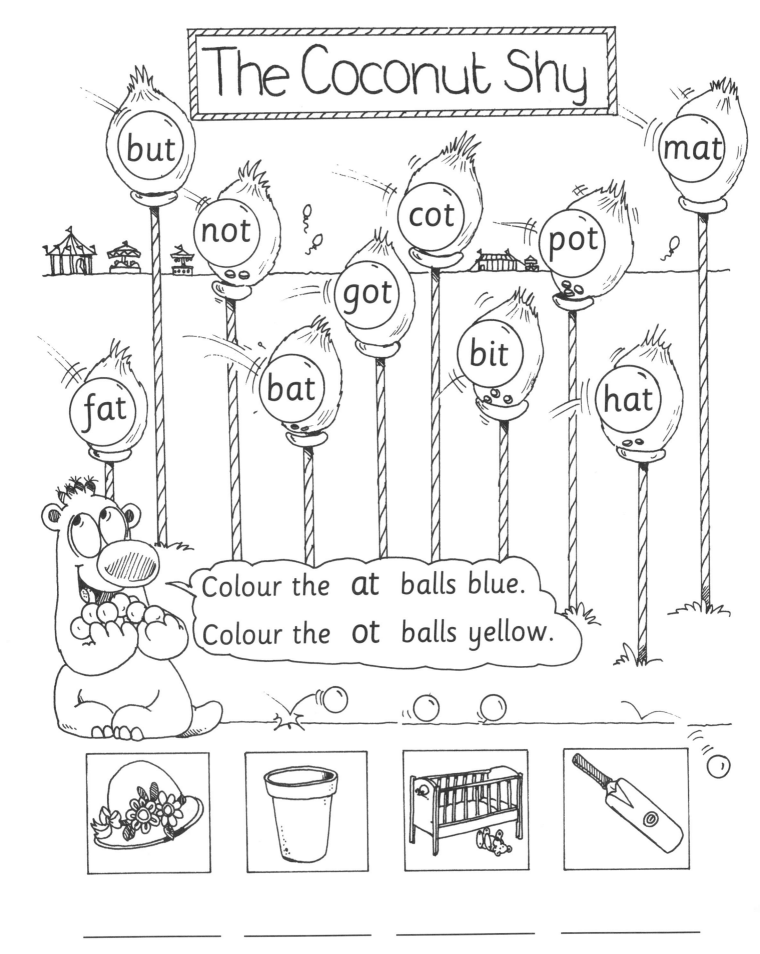

but
mat
not
cot
pot
got
bat
bit
fat
hat

Colour the **at** balls blue.
Colour the **ot** balls yellow.

Write one of the words under each picture.

Choose a letter for each ball to make a word.

Make a word	Write the word

Cover

○ at

○ at

○ at

○ ot

○ ot

○ ot

Finish the sentences with **at** or **ot** words.

This is my _____ .

My baby sleeps in a _____ .

21

Choose some letters to go here.

Make a word		Write the word
	et	
	et	
	et	
	et	
	it	
	it	
	it	
	it	

Cover

a	z	b	e	t	c
l	i	t	d	e	f
g	w	e	t	h	j
k	l	m	h	i	t
p	i	t	g	e	t

Ring the et and the it words.

23

 Good

 # Progress page

OK   Not so good

Finish the face and colour the flag for each page you have done so far.

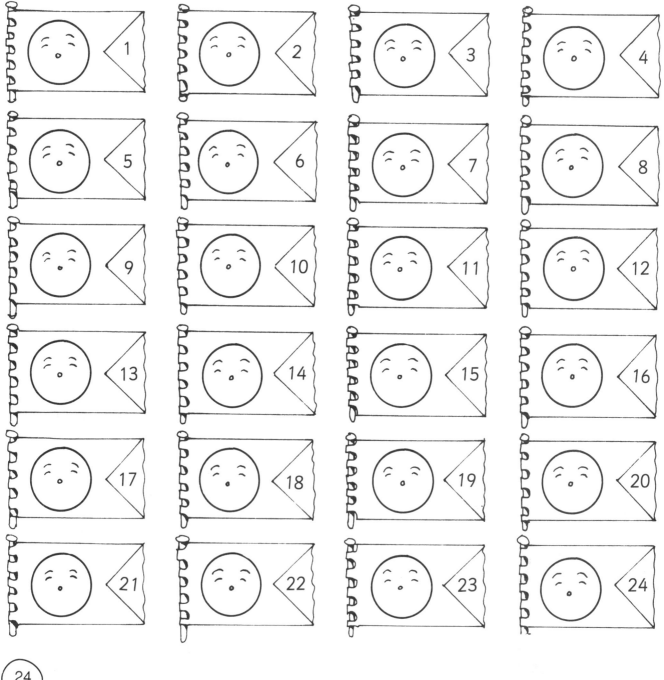

24

Spelling Workbook

Part 2

Colour in the name of the theme park.

DREAMLAND

I can see the word **am** hidden in Dreamland. Write down any words that you can find.

Bubbles

Make a word in each bubble.
Write it underneath.

c
f
h

s
b
m

r
t
g

_f_ un

fun

__ op

__ at

__ at

__ un

__ op

__ op

__ at

__ un

Colour the op bubbles red,
the at bubbles blue and
the un bubbles green.

Catch the bubbles

Look at the words in the big bubble.

cat bin pin
fit rat sit
tin bit
fat

Write the **at** words here

Write the **in** words here

Write the **it** words here

Add one more rhyming word to each group of bubbles.

Pin the tails on the donkeys

Join the right tail to each donkey to make a word.
Write the words underneath.

ix eg ug

s _____ p _____ j _____

_____ _____ _____

Write some words that rhyme on each of us.

fix leg hug
mix _____ _____ _____

_____ _____ _____

Animal tails

Join the right tail to each animal and write both words in the boxes.

Write some words that rhyme on the tails of these animals.

The big wheel

Colour the br cars brown and the gr cars green.

green brown bring grass grunt brick brush grab grip bread

Now write the br words in the br queue and the gr words in the gr queue.

br words queue here

gr words queue here

The crazy train

Write the **cr** words in the **cr** carriages and the **tr** words in the **tr** carriages.

trap	crust	crack
crash	trunk	trip
truck		crisp

Crazy train

Colour the **cr** carriages yellow and the **tr** carriages blue.

Write a sentence using a **cr** word and a **tr** word.

Roll a ball

Follow the path of each ball to make the words.

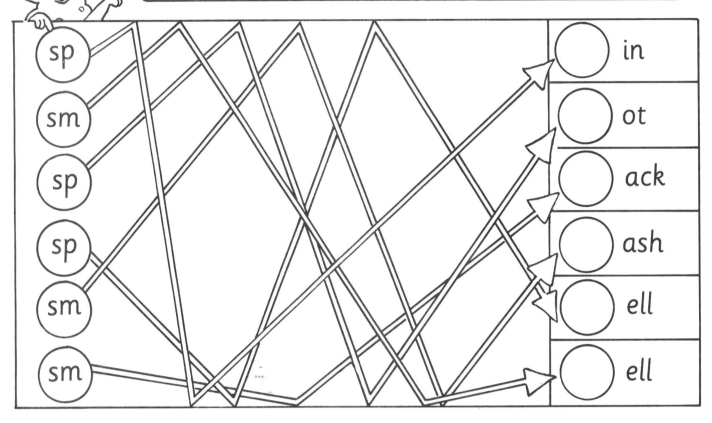

Make some more words.

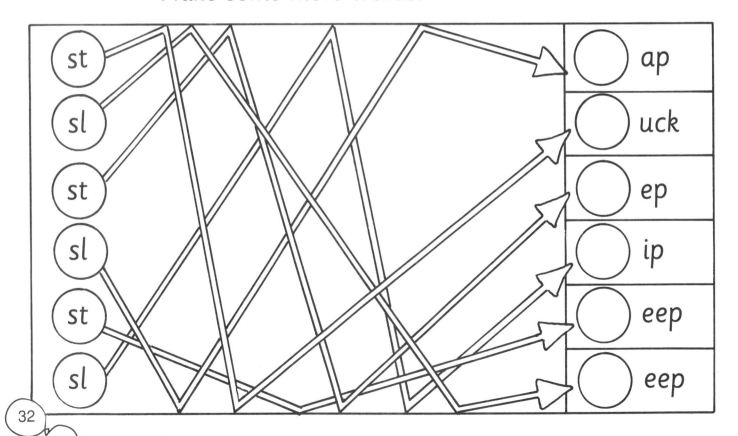

Roll a ball rhyme

Make the words and find a rhyme.

sp → sp in ⇒ spin _____

sp → ○ ot ⇒ _____

sp → ○ ell ⇒ _____

sm → ○ ack ⇒ _____

sm → ○ ash ⇒ _____

sm → ○ ell ⇒ _____

sl → ○ ap ⇒ _____

sl → ○ ip ⇒ _____

sl → ○ eep ⇒ _____

st → ○ uck ⇒ _____

st → ○ ep ⇒ _____

st → ○ eep ⇒ _____

Throw the sponge

Add **ch** and **sh** to make the words.

ch icken

chicken

___ ell

___ ips

___ erry

___ ip

ch

sh

Write these **ch** and **sh** words in the right piles.

shot   shop   chocolate   chop   shed   cheese

34

Add **ch** and **sh** to make the words.

fi _____

tor _____

pun _____

bru _____

ch	sh

Write these **ch** and **sh** words in the right piles.

rush   such   smash   wish   rich   much

35

Treasure trail

Walk around the treasure trail.
Underline the **th** words.
Circle the **wh** words.

Start here

thick

who

wheel

there

they

when

where

thank

white

why

thief

this

then

what

thin

This way to buried word treasure

ere
o
ich
y
is
en
ank
ere
in
ief
ite
ey
eel
en
at
en

Do these buried words start with **th** or **wh** ?
Write the words in the treasure chests.

th words only

thin

wh words only

Chair lift

Pick up an ending for each chair to finish the word. Write the words underneath.

ft mp nd

po __
_____

gi __
_____

bu __
_____

sa __
_____

li __
_____

da __
_____

ha __
_____

so __
_____

ju __
_____

39

Hoopla

Colour the hoops and then write the words.

Colour the words ending in **ng** green.
Colour the **nk** words red and
the **st** words yellow.

sink

junk

fast

bang

rest

wink

best

king

long

Write the **nk** words here

Write the **ng** words here

Write the **st** words here

nk

ng

st

Make a word

Cover

Write the word

Ride on the slide

Use these endings to finish the words on the mats.

n _____

g _____

r _____

s _____

sm _____

h _____

j _____

c _____

str _____

t _____

Now sort out the mats.
Colour the **ube** mats red, the **oke** mats blue, the **ide** mats green and the **ame** mats yellow.

| came | tube | joke | hide | name | poke | ride |

Write the words here.

s ____

c ____

w ____

p ____

ame

ide

oke

ube

cube | stroke | side | same | smoke | wide | game

43

Frisbees

Throw the frisbees to make the words.
You can use each ending twice.

__ oon

m ____

s ____

__ oop

h ____

l ____

__ oot

f ____

r ____

__ ood

g ____

w ____

__ ook

b ____

t ____

__ ool

c ____

p ____

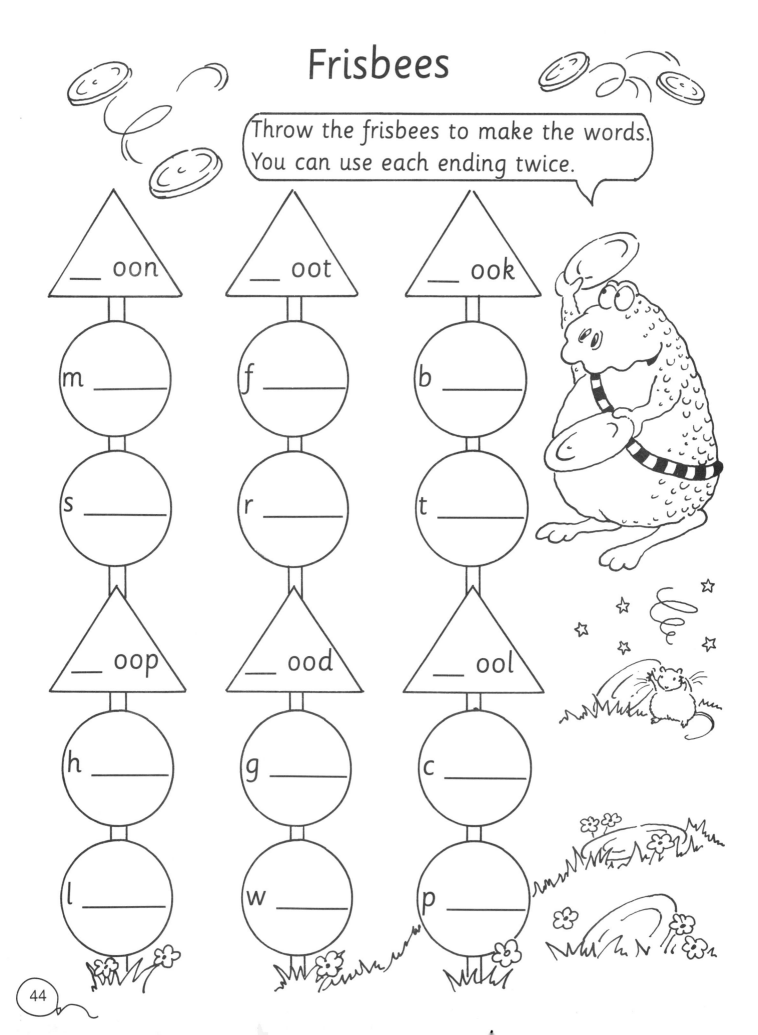

Write the words you have made.

moon

Now colour the frisbees on this page so that each word ending is in a different colour.

Jaws

Use ar or ee to
make the words.

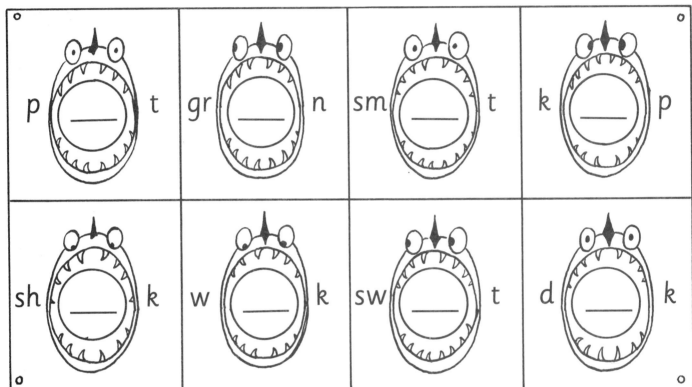

p ___ t   gr ___ n   sm ___ t   k ___ p

sh ___ k   w ___ k   sw ___ t   d ___ k

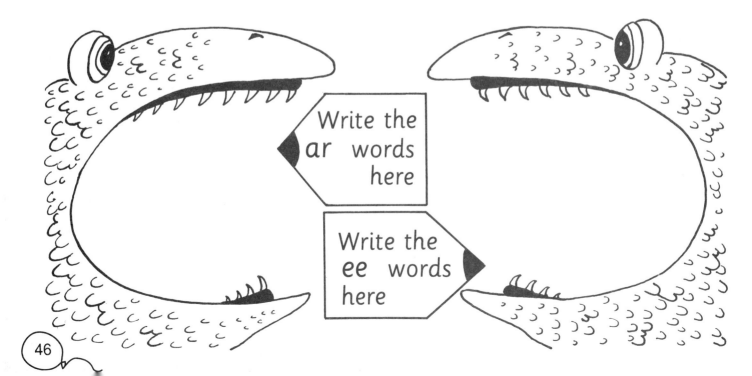

Write the
ar words
here

Write the
ee words
here

Fountain rhymes

Pick a ball to rhyme with the word in the fountain.
Write the word in the space.

heat

boat

seat

goat

house

mouse

day

play

Now make up your own rhyme!
Write a word in the ball to rhyme with the word in the fountain.

round

load

peach

way

Finish the face and colour the flag for each page.

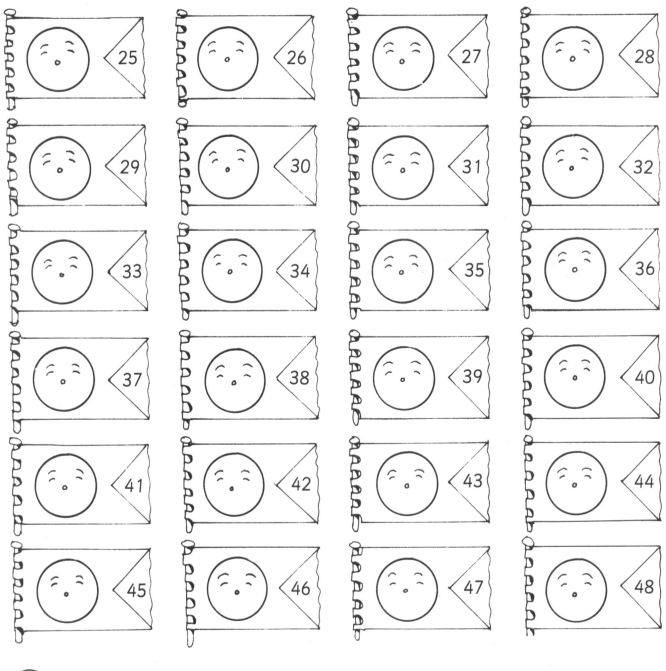